CHARACTERS FROM THE 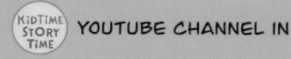 YOUTUBE CHANNEL IN

I want to be in a Book

By Dan G.

Illustrated by
Dan G. and Eliana

For Doug the Dinosaur

▶

and anyone who wants to make their
dreams come true

0:44 / 8:48

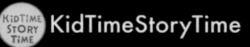 KidTimeStoryTime

Scan QR code with your phone to read along with our video!

Doug loves to read books with Storyteller and his friends. He loves to talk about books, listen to books and he would even…

dream about books.
One day Doug had a dream that he was even
IN a book

Doug looked through every book he could find about

dinosaurs

and dragons,

and half-Dinosaurs/half-Dragons

Even though Doug looked and looked,

He couldn't find himself in a book.

This book about Sergeant Perry the police pelican is fascinating!

And this made Doug sad,
because Doug really, really wanted to be in a book.

Then Doug went to go find some paper
and some colored pencils.

Doug thought and thought, but he couldn't think of a story. He had writer's block, or maybe it was thinker's block? So Doug decided that maybe he could draw the pictures first.

Doug liked to draw, but he had never made a self-portrait before, so he worked hard and took his time. Sometimes he had to start over or use his eraser but finally...

Green Bear thought that the drawing was a
HOOT
Doug
and
GreenBear

"How are we going to get there?" asked Doug.
"In a school bus!" said Green Bear.
"I've always wanted to ride in a school bus!" said Doug
So Doug drew a school bus.

That's a lot of drawing, thought Doug,
but just then he got an idea!
Doug sketched onto one of his drawings
and then showed it to his friends.

Doug quickly drew her in the front of the bus and said...

"And guess what everybody?" asked Doug.
Doug quickly drew some musical notes around the
bus and said, "We're singing the Wheels on the
Bus go round and round!"

Make your own KidTime STORYTime paper puppets!

Instructions:
With help from an adult,
1 Carefully cut out this page from book.
2 Using scissors, cut out paper puppets along the dotted lines.
3 Trace the outline of the puppet onto a piece of cardstock or cardboard. Then cut that out.
4 Glue together cardstock to the back of paper puppet!
5 Let glue dry.
6 Tape a pencil or popsicle stick to the back of paper puppet. like this!
7. HAVE FUN

You can read your favorite books with Storyteller, Doug the Dinosaur and Green Bear!

Remember to give your puppets a special voice. la la

Tip:

Made in the USA
Monee, IL
22 April 2023

32269840R00017